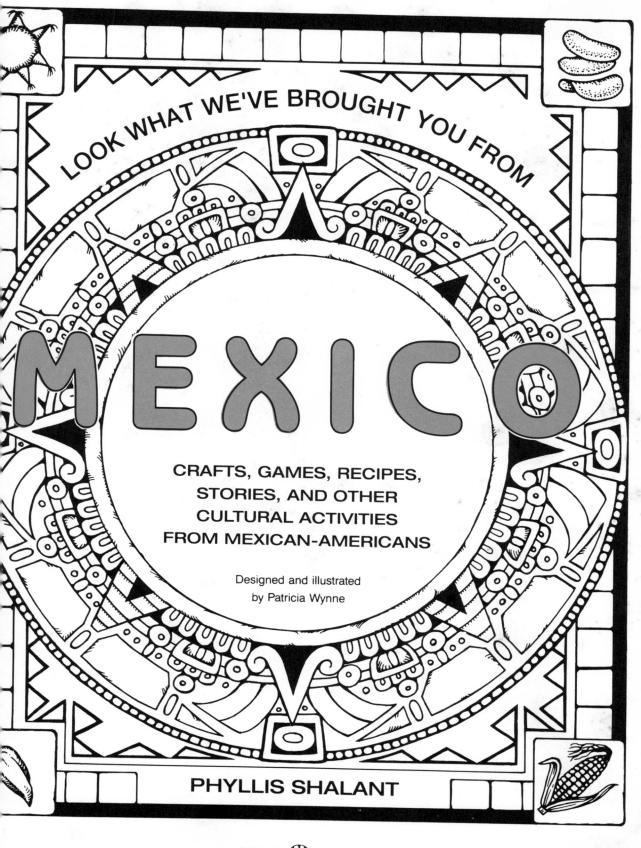

LOOK WHAT WE'VE BROUGHT YOU FROM

MEXICO

CRAFTS, GAMES, RECIPES, STORIES, AND OTHER CULTURAL ACTIVITIES FROM MEXICAN-AMERICANS

Designed and illustrated
by Patricia Wynne

PHYLLIS SHALANT

JULIAN Ⓜ MESSNER

On the front cover: An illustration based on the Aztec calendar stone

On the back cover: Breaking the piñata

Copyright © 1992 by Phyllis Shalant

Illustrations © 1992 by Patricia Wynne

JULIAN MESSNER and colophon are trademarks of Simon & Schuster

10 9 8 7 6 5 4 3 2 1 Lib. ed.
10 9 8 7 6 5 4 3 2   Paper ed.

**Library of Congress
Cataloging-in-Publication Data**

Shalant, Phyllis.
  Look what we've brought you from Mexico/Phyllis Shalant.
      p. cm.
  Includes bibliographical references and index.
  Summary: Introduces Mexican culture using crafts, recipes, games, and folktales.
  1. Mexico—Social life and customs—Juvenile literature.
2. Tales—Mexico—Juvenile literature. 3. Folklore—Mexico—Juvenile literature.
[1. Mexico—Social life and customs. 2. Cookery, Mexican. 3. Handicrafts. 4. Folklore—Mexico.]
I. Title.
F1210.S53 1992   91-43670
972—dc20   CIP
                                   AC

ISBN 0-671-75256-1 (lib. bdg.)
ISBN 0-671-75257-X (pbk.)

ACKNOWLEDGMENTS

The information in this book comes both from private individuals and public sources. Special thanks are due to the Urruchua family who gave generously of their knowledge and time. Suggestions and information from the Cultural Department of the Consulate General of Mexico in New York City were most helpful. The American Forum for Global Education allowed me access to their collection of books and materials. Mary Slamin and Mary Burnap, children's librarians at the Greenburgh Public Library in Elmsford, New York, ferreted out every book that might possibly assist me with my research. Juanita Schwartz and Frances Shalant helped with the tortilla and quesadilla recipes in this book. Jenny Shalant and Marisa Suvannavejh made the Mexican hot chocolate by themselves and drank it, too. To all of you I offer my sincere appreciation. It was fun!

Pottery dog

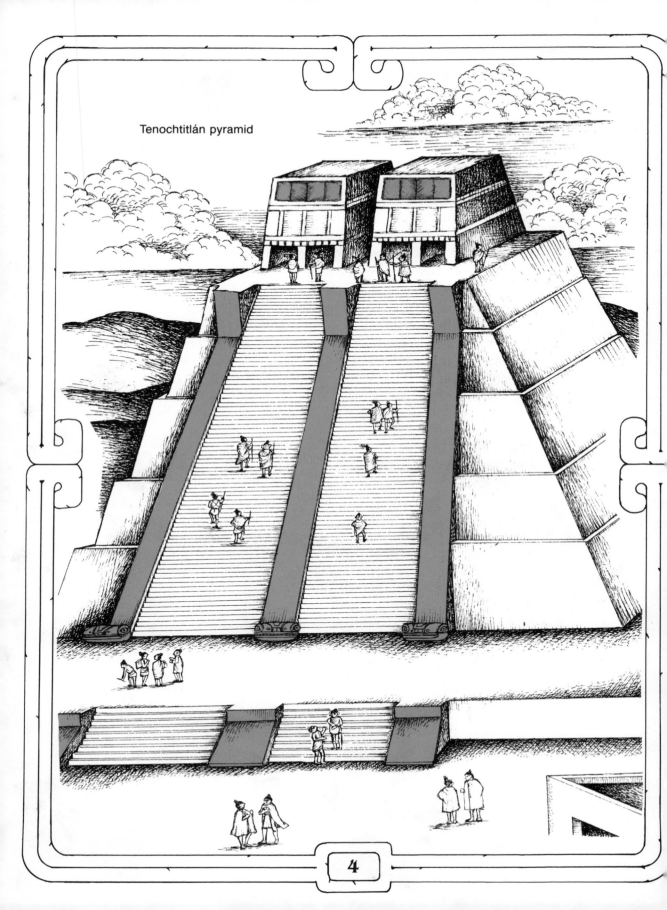

Tenochtitlán pyramid

CONTENTS

INTRODUCTION

Bite into a chocolate bar and what country do you think of? Switzerland? Belgium? France? Like most people, you'll probably be surprised to learn that chocolate is actually a gift to the world from the Indians of ancient Mexico.

Today, we take for granted many other contributions from Mexican history and culture, as well. For example, the first rubber balls were used in the ancient Mexican game of *tlachtli*. Although we usually associate pyramids with the ancient Egyptians, the Indians of Mexico built them too. Even everyday words we use in English, like *cafeteria*, *patio*, *rodeo*, *macho*, *marina*, *poncho*, *tornado*, *tomato*, and *alligator*, come to us from the Spanish and Indian languages of Mexico.

What's more, the United States and Mexico share a two-thousand-mile border that stretches all the way from Texas to Tijuana. No wonder so much of Mexico's culture has spread north! And culture is not the only part of Mexico to have traveled. According to the 1990 census, 13,495,938 Mexican-Americans now reside in the United States—about five percent of the total United States population.

If you live in the southwestern United States where ninety percent of Mexican-Americans reside, you may know a bit about their culture already. Perhaps you have Mexican-American schoolmates or neighbors. The largest Mexican-American communities are in Los Angeles and San Antonio. About eighty-five percent of Mexican-Americans live in urban areas.

Mexican-American children have games and crafts and snacks and stories to share. This book will help you get to know them a little better. *¡Que te diviertas!* Have fun!

Mayan kings

THIS IS MEXICO

Mexico is 758,136 square miles in area, about one-fourth the size of the United States. Its major land regions—the Pacific Northwest, the Plateau of Mexico, the Gulf Coastal Plain, the Chiapas Highlands, and the Yucatán Peninsula—contain an amazing variety of land and water forms, including rivers, lakes, deserts, tropical rain forests, beaches, jungles, volcanoes, mountains, and canyons.

The country, officially called *Estados Unidos Mexicanos* (United Mexican States), is divided into thirty-one states and one federal district. About two-thirds of the population live in cities and large towns with the greatest number, *over ten million*, residing in the capital, Mexico City. Located in the Plateau of Mexico region, Mexico City is the largest city in the world and the most ancient settlement in the Americas.

Pacific Northwest

Gulf Coastal Plain

Plateau
of
Mexico

Mexico City

Popocatépetl
and Ixtacihuatl

Chiapas Highlands

Yucatán
Peninsula

ANCIENT MEXICO

Ancient Mexico was inhabited by a series of Indian peoples, some of whom developed amazingly advanced and complex civilizations. These cultures flourished in a region we now call Mesoamerica, which includes the Central Plateau and spreads south to Central America. One of the earliest civilizations (1200–100 B.C.) was that of the Olmecs, known today as the "mother culture" of Mexico. The Olmecs grew corn, crushed the cacao bean to make a cocoa-like drink, and wove cotton into cloth. But they are most noted for carving giant stone heads that weighed many tons. If you visit Mexico, you can view one of these remarkable sculptures at the National Museum of Anthropology in Mexico City.

Another major civilization in Mexico was that of the Maya of the Yucatán (1500 B.C.–A.D. 900), perhaps the most brilliant of all the ancient peoples of Mesoamerica. Like the Olmecs, the Maya grew corn, which they made into little flat cornmeal cakes that later came to be called tortillas (to try making your own tortillas, see the recipe on pages 30–31). The Maya were superb architects, mathematicians, and astronomers. Their accomplishments included an accurate calendar, domed observatories, and a system of hieroglyphic writing that the Aztecs later adopted for their own (for some samples, see pages 42–43). In addition, these talented people built cities such as Uxmal, Palenque, and Chichén Itzá. But the fantastic Maya history ends in a great mystery. Why did the Maya abandon their cities around A.D. 900, leaving their civilization to practically disappear?

Ancient Mexico holds the key to another intriguing puzzle as well: Who built the legendary city that lay just thirty miles from present-day Mexico City? Spanning over twenty-five miles and populated by perhaps 150,000 people, the city that existed between A.D. 100 and 600 was probably the largest in the Western world at the time. Among its great avenues and plazas were buildings covered with fantastic paintings and a two-hundred-foot tall pyramid, the famous Pyramid of the Sun, which still stands today. Five hundred years after the city lay in ruins, it was discovered by the Aztecs, who believed such a magnificent metropolis must have been built by gods or giants. The Aztecs gave the mysterious ruined city the name *Teotihuacán*, which means "the place where those who die turn into gods."

The Aztecs themselves were a different sort of people, who arrived from the north in search of a place to establish their own civilization. In 1325, they founded their capital city, Tenochtitlán, on an island in Lake Texcoco, which lay in the Valley of Mexico. The Aztecs conquered other tribes and took thousands of slaves but they were also skillful engineers. They built aqueducts, drawbridges, and even "floating islands" to grow their crops.

When the Spanish explorer Hernán Cortés came upon the Aztecs in 1519, they had become the richest, most powerful empire in all of Mexico. The great Aztec chief Montezuma believed that Cortés was the ancient god Quetzalcóatl returned to rule his people. At first, the chief and the explorer were in awe of each other, but Cortés soon kidnapped Montezuma. The Aztecs quickly came to realize that Cortés was no god. After just two years of war, the Spanish managed to conquer and enslave the Aztecs. For nearly three hundred years thereafter, Spain ruled the land and the Indians. Finally in 1810, a parish priest named Father Miguel Hidalgo led the first of the revolts that led to independence for Mexico in 1821.

Today, the majority of the Mexican people are *mestizos*, persons of mixed Indian and Spanish ancestry. As you explore the activities in this book, you'll discover how this blend of cultures adds spice not only to Mexico's food, but also to its language, games, arts, crafts, songs, and stories.

HOLIDAY FUN

POSADAS—THE CHRISTMAS PAGEANTS OF MEXICO

Christmas is an important time in Mexico, where ninety-five percent of the people are Roman Catholic. During the nine nights before Christmas, pageants are held that tell the story of Mary and Joseph's search for an inn where Jesus could be born. Adults and children dress in biblical costumes and carry candles and statues of the holy family through the streets of their neighborhoods as they sing carols about the journey. In Spanish, the word for inn is *posada*, and that is why these processions are known as *posadas.*

As they march, the members of the procession knock at nine doors. At the first eight doors, they are sent on their way; but at the ninth, the door is opened and the fiesta begins. Songs, prayers, food, dancing, and games are all part of the evening.

For children, the highlight of *posadas* is the breaking of the *piñata,* a specially decorated container filled with treats of candy, fruit, or small toys. *Piñatas* come in many shapes and sizes and are also used to celebrate other events, but for Christmas, the traditional shape is a star.

During the holiday season, many families make their own *piñatas* and hang them as decorations until it is time to play the *piñata* game and collect the treasures inside. On the following pages, you will find instructions for making a colorful *piñata* of your own and for playing the game that leads to the breaking, the eating, and the fun.

MAKE A STAR *PIÑATA*

Celebrate Christmas Mexican-style with this treasure-filled craft. The project is ideal for group work and takes about a week to complete.

Materials:
Newspapers (several days' worth for construction and protecting work surfaces)
3-4 cups flour
Water
2 large bowls
Stirring implement, compass, ruler, scissor, stapler, marker

Round, 11" diameter balloon
Large jar of rubber cement
10-foot cord for hanging piñata
20" × 30" tissue paper (4 sheets of red, 4 sheets of green, 1 sheet of white)
12" square of aluminum foil
Masking tape
Small wrapped candies

Instructions:
Before you begin, cover your work surface with some of the newspaper. Be sure you are wearing a long smock or washable clothing you won't mind getting messy.

1. Inflate balloon and tie end. Draw a circle that is 3" in diameter around knot to mark opening of *piñata*.

2. Prepare five cone-shaped points for star: With compass, draw two 8" circles on three layers of newspaper. Cut circles into quarters and staple the three layers of each one together for easy handling. Roll five newspaper cones from quartered circles, cementing ends together. To make shiny tips of star, cut two 4" circles of foil and quarter. Cement foil onto cone tips.

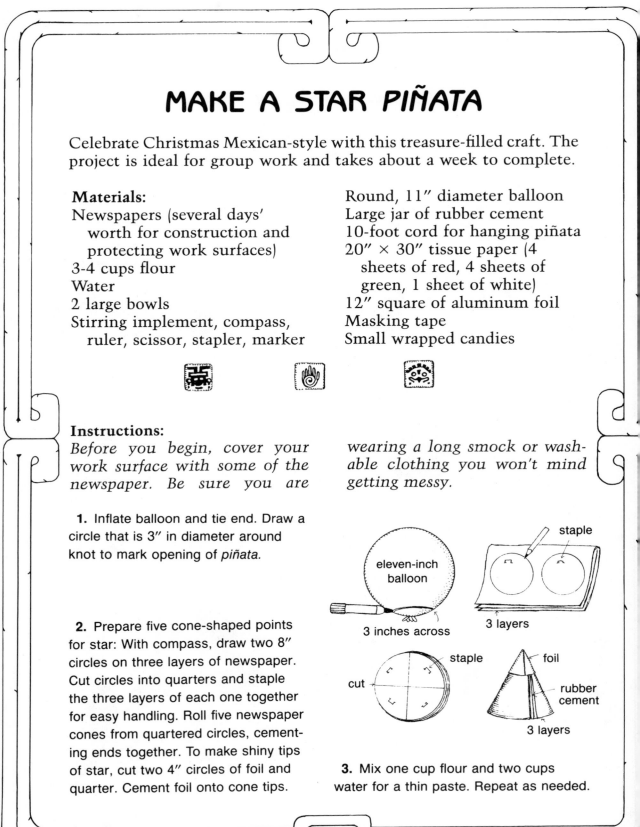

eleven-inch balloon

3 inches across

staple

3 layers

cut

staple

foil

rubber cement

3 layers

3. Mix one cup flour and two cups water for a thin paste. Repeat as needed.

4. Tear or cut newspaper into strips, approximately 2″ wide × 14″ long.

5. Dip newspaper strips into paste. Starting just below opening you have marked, cover balloon in four layers of paper. (It is not necessary to let a layer dry before applying the next one).

6. While *piñata* is still wet, attach five prepared star points by cutting 1″ notches around bottom edge of each cone, folding back as shown, and pasting them in place.

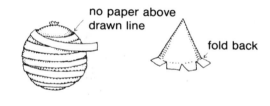

no paper above
drawn line

fold back

7. Allow 24 to 36 hours for *piñata* to dry.

8. Pop balloon. Attach cord by looping around two star points nearest the opening and weaving around each of the other three points. Use masking tape to secure cord to form, leaving about 3 feet to thread through top loops for later suspension.

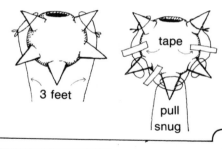

3 feet

tape

pull
snug

9. For ruffles, stack four sheets of red tissue paper, cut strips 3″ wide × 30″ long, then cut in half, so strips measure 3″×15″. Fold in half lengthwise and cut slits about 3/4″ deep and 1/4″ apart all along the folded edge, leaving about 1/2″ of uncut tissue on each end. Separate ruffle strips, refold each inside out and cement together along long edge. Ruffles should puff out. (Young children may make simple

fringed strips instead.) Cement ruffles around star's points, just above foil tips. Add each layer of ruffling close to last layer, covering portion cemented to *piñata*. When you have covered each point in red ruffles, make five white ruffles and cement just above the red ones where cones meet body. Attach ruffling over cord, as necessary. Now make enough green ruffles to cover body, exposing only opening at top.

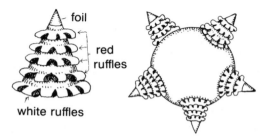

foil

red
ruffles

white ruffles

10. Fill finished *piñata* with candies. Now you are ready to play.

PIÑATA GAMES AND SONGS

For children, the breaking of the *piñata* is the highlight of the Christmas fiesta. Teasing and joking with each player are part of the game, and everyone gets a treat when the *piñata* is finally broken.

Materials:
Blindfold
Stick or bat (broom handle,
    branch, light baseball bat)
Piñata

To Set Up:
A large open space like a gym or a playground is the best place to play. You will also need a low tree branch or, if indoors, a beam or ceiling hook from which to suspend the *piñata.* An adult or older child should be chosen as the "leader" who will raise and lower the *piñata.*

To Play:
1. Leader throws the *piñata's* suspension rope over branch, beam, or hook and keeps hold of free end.
2. First player is blindfolded and spun around three times by other children. Stick or broom handle is placed in player's hand.
3. While children shout "*¡Dale! ¡dale!*" (dah-lay! dah-lay!) which means "hit it! hit it," player tries to whack *piñata.* Leader uses rope to raise and lower *piñata,* keeping it just out of reach.
4. After each child has had a turn, the second round begins. Leader lowers *piñata* within range. Only one hit is allowed per player. It may take quite a few hits before *piñata* cracks.
5. As soon as treats fall out of *piñata,* players rush to collect as many as they can.

CANCIÓN DE LA PIÑATA—PIÑATA SONG

The breaking of the *piñata* is usually accompanied by joking and singing. Here is a simple song you may wish to learn.

Piñata Song

In the hap - py days of Christ - mas, _____
En las no - ches de po - sa - das, _____

Sounds of glad - ness fill the air; _____
La pi - ña - ta es lo me - jor; _____

When it's time for the pi - ña - ta, _____
La ni - ña más re - mil - ga - da _____

There's ex - cite - ment ev - 'ry - where. _____
Se al - bo - ro - ta con ar - dor. _____

1. Take a stick and whack it, Be the one to crack it;
2. *Da - le, da - le, da - le, no pier - das el ti - no,*

Win pi - ña - ta's trea - sure, Can - dies for your plea - sure.
Que de la dis - tan - cia se pier - de el ca - mi - no.

15

EL DÍA DE LOS MUERTOS— DAY OF THE DEAD

On November second, soon after children in the United States have celebrated Halloween, the Mexican people observe a day that is also filled with the images of skeleton bones and the sweet taste of candies and cakes. But unlike Halloween, *El Día de los Muertos*, which means the Day of the Dead, is not meant for costumes and pranks. Instead it is a special occasion when families remember and honor their friends and relatives who have died.

Yet, *El Día de los Muertos* is not a sad time. On this day, bakers make their famous *pan de muerto*, or bread of the dead, delicious anise-scented loaves that are filled with raisins and decorated with crossbones made of dough or sugar icing. A favorite treat of Mexican children on *El Día de los Muertos* is the specially made *dulces*, sugary marzipan candies formed in the shape of little skulls and coffins. During the holiday, the bake shops and markets of Mexico are filled with these colorful confections.

Of course, food is not the only way that Mexican families remember their dead. On *El Día de los Muertos*, families visit the cemeteries where their loved ones are buried. There they picnic together and discuss happy memories. Often, they bring marigolds, known in Mexico as the flower of the dead, to decorate the graves. At night, the cemetery becomes aglow with flickering candles and smoky incense that loving friends and relatives have placed on the tombstones. In this way, the past is kept alive.

Skull-shaped candy

PAN DE MUERTO—
BREAD OF THE DEAD

To bake *pan de muerto*, start early in the morning because the dough must be left to rise for about two hours. This spooky bread makes a good Halloween treat.

Ingredients:
1/4 cup milk
1/4 cup (half a stick) margarine
    or butter, cut into 8 pieces
1/4 cup sugar
1/2 teaspoon salt
  1 package active dry yeast
1/4 cup very warm water
  2 eggs
  3 cups all-purpose flour,
    unsifted
1/2 teaspoon anise seed
1/4 teaspoon ground cinnamon
  2 teaspoons sugar

Utensils:
Small saucepan
Measuring cups and spoons
Large mixing bowl
Three small bowls
Mixing spoons
Pastry board or clean, smooth
  surface for kneading dough
Dish towel
Baking sheet

Directions:
When you use the oven or stove, have an adult standing by.
1. Bring milk to boil and remove from heat. Stir in butter, 1/4 cup sugar and salt.
2. In large bowl, mix yeast with warm water until dissolved and let stand five minutes. Add the milk mixture.
3. Separate the yolk and white of one egg. Add the yolk to the yeast mixture, but save the white for later. Now add another whole egg to the yeast mixture.
4. Measure the flour and add to the yeast and eggs. Blend well until dough ball is formed.

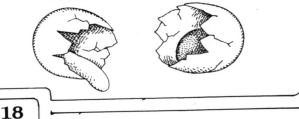

5. Flour the pastry board or work surface very well and place the dough in center. Knead until smooth. Return to large bowl and cover with dish towel. Let rise in warm place for 90 minutes. Meanwhile, grease the baking sheet and preheat the oven to 350 degrees.

6. Knead dough again on floured surface. Now divide the dough into fourths and set one aside. Roll the remaining three pieces into "ropes." On *greased* baking sheet, pinch three rope ends together and braid. Finish by pinching ends together on opposite side. Divide the remaining dough in half and form two "bones." Cross and lay them atop braided loaf.

7. Cover bread with dish towel and let rise for 30 minutes. Meanwhile, mix anise seed, cinnamon, and sugar together. Beat egg white lightly.

8. When 30 minutes are up, brush top of bread with egg white and sprinkle with sugar mixture, *except on cross bones.* Bake at 350 degrees for 35 minutes.

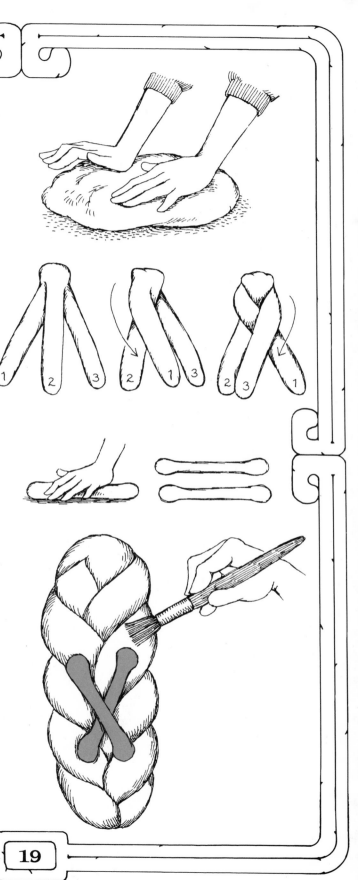

MEXICAN INDEPENDENCE DAY

"¡Mexicanos! ¡Viva Mexico! ¡Viva la Independencia!" On September 16, 1810, in the small town of Dolores just outside Mexico City, Father Miguel Hidalgo, a parish priest, rang his church bell and shouted the words that were to begin the Mexican people's fight for freedom. Although the first rebellion was quickly crushed by Spain's royal forces, the revolution had begun. The war continued for more than ten years until finally, in 1821, Mexico was declared an independent nation.

Today, on September 16th, Father Hidalgo's famous *Grito de Dolores* (Cry of Dolores) demanding independence can be heard in every city and town across Mexico. People gather on the main plazas where local officials ring their liberty bells and call *"¡Mexicanos, viva nuestros heroes!"* ("Mexicans, long live our heroes!") As each hero's name is read aloud, the crowd cheers *"¡Viva!"* The *grito* ends with the shout *"¡Viva Mexico!"* and throughout the nation, church bells toll as the people rejoice.

There is even a special dish, *chiles en nogada,* to celebrate Independence Day in Mexico. Long green chiles are stuffed with ground pork or beef and spices, dipped in batter, and fried. Then they are covered in a thick, white sauce, sprinkled with red pomegranate seeds, and topped with a sprig of parsley. What makes this dish the perfect Independence Day meal? Its colors are green, white, and red, just like Mexico's flag!

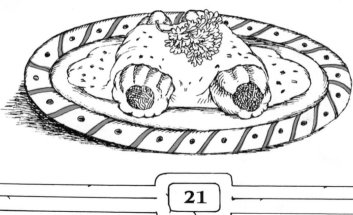

CREATE A MURAL FOR INDEPENDENCE DAY

Mexico is well known for its murals, giant wall paintings that use pictures to tell stories of both the past and the present. Although mural painting in Mexico is very much alive today, it was popular among the ancient Maya and Aztecs as well. In fact, one of the oldest known murals in existence (A.D. 700) is at the Maya temple of Bonampak in the state of Chiapas.

Diego Rivera, a twentieth-century artist, studied the ancient murals. He learned how the Aztecs used insect oils, sap, and natural earth colors to produce their traditional colors of red, green, yellow, and turquoise. Rivera became the most celebrated mural artist of his country.

Today the works of Rivera and other muralists cover the walls of many public buildings. These murals show Aztec pyramids and Olmec sculptures, heroes of the revolution, religious events, and current scenes of life on farms and in the cities. They help to develop the Mexican people's awareness of, and pride in, their heritage.

Materials:
4 or more feet of brown craft paper
Tempera paint: red, green, yellow, white, and blue
Brushes, water, bowls for mixing and rinsing
Masking tape, pencils, erasers

Instructions:
To eliminate drips, it is best to lay out your paper on the floor for painting, and hang it on the wall later when it is dry. Before you begin, cover the floor with newspaper and yourself with a smock.

1. Review the information on ancient Mexico (pages 8–9) and on Mexican Independence Day (pages 20–21). You might also want to look ahead to the hieroglyphs (pages 42–43). Decide which parts of Mexico's heritage you want to show. If you are working with a group, divide up the scenes.
2. Sketch your scenes in pencil first, covering as much of the paper as you can. If your mural will be telling a story, make sure its sequence is correct; for example, the ancient Indians should come before the Spaniards.
3. Paint in your sketches.
4. When it is dry, hang your finished mural on a wall with the masking tape.

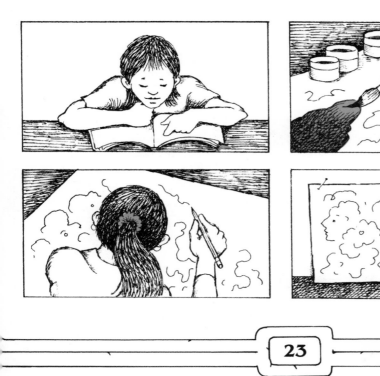

FOLKTALES AND LEGENDS

POPOCATÉPETL AND IXTACIHUATL

Southeast of Mexico City lie two of Mexico's best known volcanoes. Popocatépetl means "smoking mountain" in Aztec, and although this snow-topped volcano has not erupted since 1943, it still belches great clouds of smoke and gas into the sky. About 11 miles away from Popocatépetl, or "Popo" as the people call it, lies Ixtacihuatl, the "sleeping woman," a volcano named because its three snowy peaks make it appear like a giant woman who has lain down for a nap. There are many stories about how these famous volcanoes came to be. This is one version.

Beautiful Princess Ixtacihuatl fell in love with the soldier Popocatépetl. The two wanted to marry, but the king said that first Popocatépetl must earn his daughter's hand by fighting invaders from foreign lands. While Popo was away, many suitors tried to win the hand of the lovely maiden, but Ixtacihuatl refused them all.

Day after day, Ixtacihuatl tended her garden and watched the road for Popocatépetl to return. One day a soldier passing by saw her in the garden and wanted her for his wife. "I cannot marry you, for I am promised to a brave warrior," Ixtacihuatl told him.

"What is the name of your betrothed?" the soldier asked.

"He is Popocatépetl." Just saying his name made Ixtacihuatl smile.

"Then wait no more, for Popocatépetl died in battle," the soldier told her. "You will be my wife instead."

But Ixtacihuatl refused to marry the soldier. Instead, she climbed the mountain that rose from the foot of her garden. When she reached the top, she lay down and wept. In the night, snow began to fall upon Ixtacihuatl, but still she stayed and grieved. The snow fell for many nights until the maiden was covered and her crying could be heard no more.

One day, a brave warrior came walking down the road and stopped at Ixtacihuatl's gate. "Where is my bride-to-be?" he wondered, for it was Popocatépetl. He was not dead after all. The soldier who had spoken to Ixtacihuatl had lied, hoping to trick her into marrying him.

The neighbors came and gathered around Popocatépetl. "Ixtacihuatl is there now," they said, pointing to the mountain. "She died mourning for her true love."

Popocatépetl climbed the tall mountain that overshadowed the smaller Ixtacihuatl. There he lit a candle to watch over his true love and waited for the snow to fall. Soon he too was covered and became one with the mountain. The lovers are there still.

THE LEGEND OF QUETZALCÓATL

Few legends actually come to life, but for a brief time, it seemed as if an Aztec myth did become real. The ancient Indians worshipped many gods. One of them, Quetzalcóatl, was the god of wind, wisdom, and goodness. His name came from a combination of two Aztec words, *quetzal*, which means bird of paradise, and *cóatl*, which means serpent. In their paintings, the Aztecs showed Quetzalcóatl costumed in a feather headdress and a serpent mask.

The Aztecs believed that Quetzalcóatl was tall, light-skinned, and bearded. This peaceful, intelligent god lived among his people as a man and taught them many things including weaving, pottery, how to grind corn, and create a calendar. But Quetzalcóatl had a warlike brother, Smoking Mirror, who wanted the Indians to fear the gods. He chased Quetzalcóatl to the edge of the earth, where the gentle god carved a canoe to carry him over the ocean. Before Quetzalcóatl sailed away, he promised his people that he would return to them in the year 1-Reed.

Indian priests studied their calendars to learn when 1-Reed would fall. In our calendar, it would have been the equivalent of either the year 1467 or the year 1519. But 1467 passed without the arrival of the god, and so 1519 became the year the Aztecs believed Quetzalcóatl would finally return.

In 1519 a tall, light-skinned, bearded man did arrive by sea! This man was Hernán Cortés the explorer. The Aztecs, however, believed that he must be Quetzalcóatl. They welcomed him with gifts and honors, but the explorer and his troops were greedy. They wanted more than treasure—they wanted the Indians' land itself. When the Aztecs realized that Cortés was only a man, they began to resist the Spanish troops. Although the Indians fought bravely, Cortés and his followers soon conquered the Aztec civilization.

Ground corn

Metate

LET'S EAT!

When the Spanish explorers arrived in Mexico, the Indians introduced them to many unfamiliar foods, including tomatoes, squash, avocadoes, pineapple, chocolate, numerous varieties of beans and peppers, and the most important ingredient of Mexican cooking, corn. In fact, to the Maya, corn was actually sacred. *Popol Vuh*, their holy book, states that man was created from maize, or native corn.

From corn, the ancient Mexicans created the *tortilla*—a flat, round, bread-like food. The first tortillas were made of dried corn kernels stored by the Indians after their harvest. These kernels were softened in water with lime and then ground by hand on a stone mortar called a *metate.* The moist meal known as *masa* was then patted into a thin pancake and baked on a clay griddle called a *comal.*

In some parts of the country, tortillas are still made the ancient way, but modern cooks buy ready-made masa dough to bake at home or fresh tortillas from a *tortilleria.* No matter how it's made though, the handy tortilla is served at almost every meal. It may be used in place of utensils to scoop up other edibles, or as a plate on which other foods are piled, or toasted or fried, or rolled or folded or stuffed. No wonder the tortilla has been popular for hundreds of years!

Today, tortillas are eaten all over the world. In the United States, you can find them in many local supermarkets. But if you would like to make your own tortillas, you can use *masa harina*, a special tortilla flour that is available in grocery stores that carry Mexican products. A simple recipe is given on the following page.

Masa

Comal

CORN TORTILLAS

Ingredients:
2 cups masa harina (dehydrated masa flour)
1 cup warm water

Utensils:
Heavy frying pan or griddle
Large mixing bowl
Measuring cups
Waxed paper
Glass or ceramic pie plate
Spatula

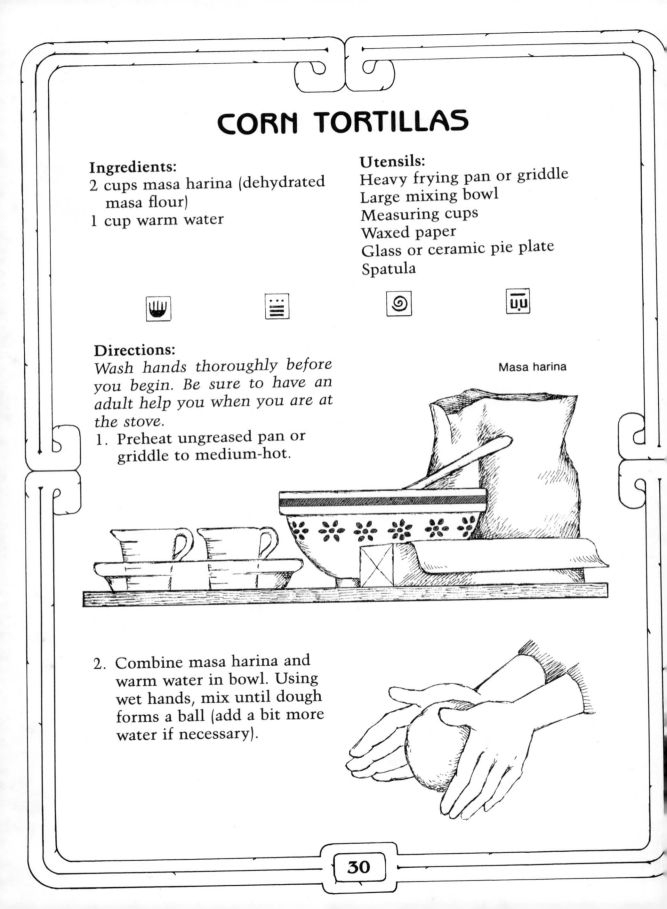

Directions:
Wash hands thoroughly before you begin. Be sure to have an adult help you when you are at the stove.

1. Preheat ungreased pan or griddle to medium-hot.

Masa harina

2. Combine masa harina and warm water in bowl. Using wet hands, mix until dough forms a ball (add a bit more water if necessary).

3. Wet hands again and shape dough into twelve smaller balls (about the size of golf balls). Cover bowl with waxed paper to keep balls moist.

4. Tear off two 9″ sheets of waxed paper. Place one masa ball between waxed paper sheets and press flat with bottom of pie plate to create thin circle, approximately 6″ in diameter.

5. Peel off top sheet of waxed paper. Flip over and drop tortilla, paper side up, onto pan or griddle. Peel off remaining paper as tortilla warms up. Cook for 30 seconds on first side. Turn. Cook one minute on second side. Turn for 30 seconds more. Tortilla should be soft and dry, with light brown flecks.

Yield: 12 servings

QUESADILLAS— TORTILLAS WITH CHEESE

Quesadillas are like little Mexican pizzas. They begin with dough and cheese, but whatever else you put on them is up to your tastebuds and your imagination. The ingredients below include some suggestions.

Ingredients:
1 tortilla per person (see pages 30–31 for recipe, or purchase ready-made at supermarket)

1/4 cup shredded mild cheese for each tortilla (Suggestions: cheddar, Monterey Jack, American, Swiss, mozzarella)

Few pieces of mild jalapeño peppers, chopped or diced (optional)

Sliced, pitted olives (optional)

Tomato, chopped (optional)

Onion, chopped (optional)

1 tsp. mild salsa (optional) *This is a tomato and chile sauce available in most supermarkets.*

Utensils:
Cheese grater
Paring knife
Cutting board
Oven or toaster oven
Baking tray
Pot holder or mitt

Directions:

Have an adult present when you are using the oven. Always use an oven mitt to handle hot trays.

1. Preheat oven to 350 degrees.
2. Heat tortilla lightly on tray in oven until warm.
3. Sprinkle cheese over warm tortilla and bake until melted. Remove from oven.
4. Place tortilla on plate. Add toppings of your choice. Eat warm.

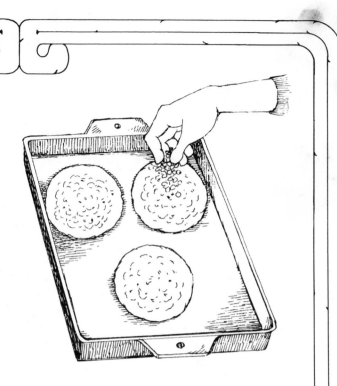

CHOCOLATE CALIENTE MEXICANO— MEXICAN HOT CHOCOLATE

What puts the 'Mexican' in Mexican hot chocolate? It is spiced with cinnamon and beaten to a froth with a *molinillo*, a decorative wooden beater that is spun between the palms. You may be able to find thick, round "coins" of Mexican chocolate in a grocery that carries Mexican food products. This special chocolate already contains the cinnamon you'll need for the recipe that follows. But you can also make this delicious drink by adding cinnamon to any bar of semi-sweet or milk chocolate.

Ingredients:
6 ounces of plain, sweetened chocolate or Mexican chocolate
6 cups milk (preferably whole milk)
1-1/2 teaspoons cinnamon (unless you are using Mexican chocolate)

Utensils:
Measuring cup
2-quart saucepan
Measuring spoons
Molinillo or eggbeater

Molinillo

Cinnamon

Milk

Directions:
Make sure an adult is present when you are using the stove.

1. Combine chocolate, milk, and cinnamon (if necessary) in saucepan.

Chocolate pieces

2. Cook over very low heat, stirring constantly until chocolate is completely melted.

3. Remove from heat. Using molinillo or eggbeater, beat until foamy. Serve hot.

Yield: Six servings

INDIAN KICKBALL

This exciting team game combines racing, kicking, and ingenuity. In northern Mexico, the Tarahumara Indians hold kickball races between local villages and race day is a special occasion. Teams of six players each kick a carved oak ball about three inches in diameter over a course that stretches from twenty to forty miles. But in this version, you can lay out a route in a playground, a field, or in your school gymnasium. For smaller spaces, your course can be shaped like a figure eight.

Equipment:

2 rubber balls, approximately 3″ in diameter; one painted with a red stripe and the other with a blue stripe

Boards and bricks to create ramps

Cardboard boxes, road cones, rocks, and other objects to create obstacles

Three or more coffee cans (open on both ends) taped together to create a tunnel

Chalk, masking tape, and/or pebbles, scissors

Note: The more ramps, tunnels, obstacles, and twists on your course, the more fun the game will be!

Tarahumara kickball racers

To Set Up:

1. Decide on the start and finish lines of your race course and mark with a line of tape or pebbles.

2. Along the route, set up ramps using boards propped up by stones or bricks. Create and position tunnels by cutting out bottoms of coffee cans and taping

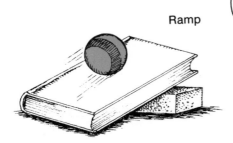

Ramp

several cans together with masking tape. Put stones or bricks on either side of "tunnel" to keep it from rolling. Use road cones, cardboard boxes, chairs, etc., for obstacles on your course. Designing the course is half the fun!

To Play:

1. Each team (red and blue) should be made up of no less than two and no more than six players, depending on size of race course. Smaller courses will be too crowded with the larger number of players.

2. Two referees are designated, one for each team. Players should watch while one referee walks the course, pointing out obstacles, ramps, tunnels, and twists in route.

3. One player on each team is designated first kicker. At referee's call, the first kicker on each team kicks the ball as far as possible along the course. Team members run after their ball, kicking it

along, and making sure to keep their ball as close to the route as possible. Each team's referee follows along, making sure ball goes through tunnels, over ramps, and around obstacles. No short cuts are permitted.

4. No team member may kick the ball more than twice in a row. Team members should cooperate.

5. Team members may not kick their opponents' ball away from course.

6. The first team to kick the ball across the finish line wins the game.

Coffee can tunnel

DOÑA BLANCA

This traditional circle game is played by children all over Mexico. It can be held indoors or out, and there is no limit on the number of players as long as there are enough children to form a comfortable circle. The words may be sung or chanted while the chase goes on.

In Spanish:
Doña Blanca está cubierta
con pilares de oro y plata.
Romperemos un pilar
Para ver a Doña Blanca.

¡Quién es ese Jicotillo
que anda en pos de Doña Blanca?
¡Yo soy ése, yo soy ése
que anda en pos de Doña Blanca!

In English:
Doña Blanca all surrounded
By pillars silver and gold
Break a column now
If Doña Blanca you will hold.

Who is this hornet
Who chases Doña Blanca?
I am (s)he, I am (s)he
Who's trying to catch her!

To Play:

1. Choose a *Doña Blanca* and a *Jicotillo.* Other children form circle. Doña Blanca stands inside ring and Jicotillo remains on the outside.
2. Children join hands and circle around Doña Blanca as they sing or chant. After second verse, Jicotillo tries to break through clasped hands to catch Doña Blanca.
3. When Jicotillo succeeds in entering circle, (s)he chases Doña Blanca until she is caught. (Doña Blanca may not run outside circle).
4. When she has been caught, Doña Blanca chooses new Jicotillo before she becomes part of circle. Jicotillo becomes new Doña Blanca.

A LA VÍBORA DE LA MAR—
THE SEA SERPENT

The sea serpent winds its way over the ocean and passes through an underwater cave. Although the words are very different, this playground game is actually a lot like "London Bridge." The longer the serpent's tail, the more fun the game! Who will get through—and who will get caught?

In Spanish:
A la víbora, víbora de la mar, de la mar,
por aquí pueden pasar;
los de adelante corren mucho,
y los de atrás se quedarán.

¡Tras, tras, tras, tras!

Una mexicana,
¡qué fruta vendía!
Ciruela, chabacano,
melón o sandía.

Día, día, día,
¡será la vieja del otro día!

Verbena, verbena,
jardín de matatena.

Campanita de oro,
déjame pasar
con todos mis hijos,
¡menos el de atrás!

¡Tras, tras, tras, tras!

In English:

The serpent, serpent of the sea
can pass through here, through here;
The ones in front run very fast,
those in back get left behind.

Behind, behind, behind, behind!

A Mexican girl,
what did she sell?
Plums or apricots,
cantaloupes or watermelons.

Day, day, day,
It must be the old woman of the other day!

Verbena, verbena,
in a garden of jacks.

Little bell of gold,
let me pass
With all my children,
except the last!

Behind, behind, behind, behind!

To Play:

1. Two players are chosen to be the "cave." They face each other, holding hands; their arms are raised to allow the serpent to pass between them.
2. Other children line up to form the serpent and pass through the cave as they chant the words to the game. At the phrase *"Tras, tras, tras, tras!"* (Behind, behind, behind, behind!), the players who are acting as the cave drop their arms and catch whomever is between them.
3. The child who is caught takes the place of one member of the cave, and that player joins the end of the serpent.

MEXICAN MIND-WORK

WRITE LIKE THE AZTECS

Aztec writing, like their calendar and numbers, was based on Mayan models. Instead of an alphabet, both groups used picture symbols known as hieroglyphs. These symbols stood for words and phrases in the Aztec's spoken language. The Aztecs carved their hieroglyphs on the steps of their temples and on stone monuments called stelae. They even produced paper from fig-tree bark, which they used for books of religious ceremonies, calendars, and astronomical tables.

Even today, most Aztec hieroglyphs—called glyphs for short— have not been decoded, but here are some examples of hieroglyphs for which we do know the meanings. Try to guess what they are before you check the answers on page 45.

Stelae

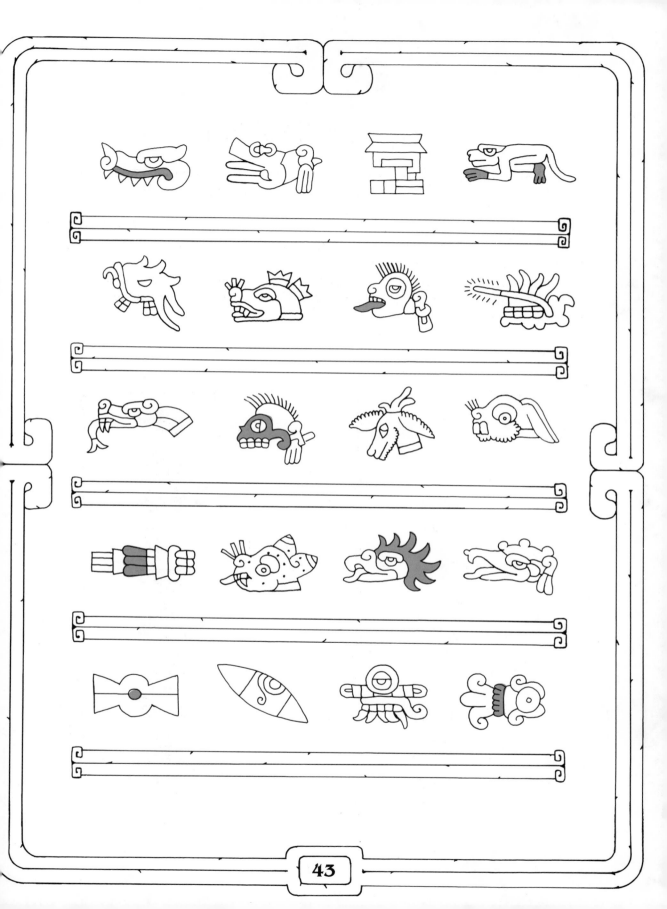

MAYAN NUMBERS

The mathematical Maya had a very clever and unusual system of numbers to do their calculations. Unlike our method, which is based on the number ten, the Mayan system was based on the number twenty. To represent numbers, they used dots and dashes, with a shell, a hand, or a head for zero. Instead of writing their numbers horizontally, the Maya wrote them vertically.

Using this chart of Mayan numbers, see if you can solve the addition and subtraction problems on page 45. Give your answers in Mayan numbers, too.

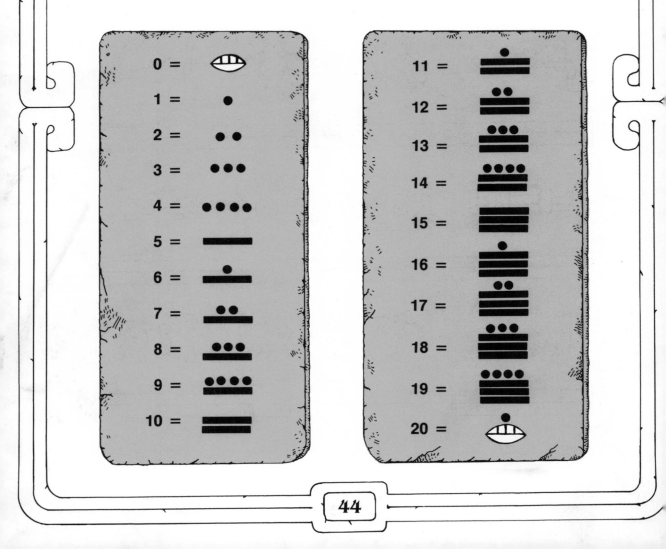